MW00964472

HOW DO THEY MAKE THAT?

TOOTHPASTE

Jan Bernard and John Willis

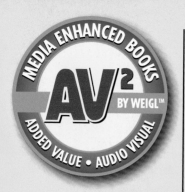

MEDIA ENHANCED BOOKS
AV²
BY WEIGL™
ADDED VALUE • AUDIO VISUAL

AV² provides enriched content that supplements and complements this book. Weigl's AV² books strive to create inspired learning and engage young minds in a total learning experience.

Your AV² Media Enhanced books come alive with...

Audio
Listen to sections of the book read aloud.

Key Words
Study vocabulary, and complete a matching word activity.

Video
Watch informative video clips.

Quizzes
Test your knowledge.

Go to **www.av2books.com**, and enter this book's unique code.

BOOK CODE

C 6 8 6 4 4 4

Embedded Weblinks
Gain additional information for research.

Slide Show
View images and captions, and prepare a presentation.

AV² by Weigl brings you media enhanced books that support active learning.

Try This!
Complete activities and hands-on experiments.

... and much, much more!

Published by AV² by Weigl
350 5th Avenue, 59th Floor
New York, NY 10118
Website: www.av2books.com

Library of Congress Cataloging-in-Publication Data

Names: Bernard, Jan, author | and Willis, John, author.
Title: Toothpaste / Jan Bernard.
Description: New York, NY : AV2 by Weigl, [2017] | Series: How do they make that? | Includes bibliographical references and index.
Identifiers: LCCN 2016005666 (print) | LCCN 2016006754 (ebook) | ISBN 9781489645470 (hard cover : alk. paper) | ISBN 9781489652621 (soft cover : alk. paper) | ISBN 9781489645487 (Multi-user ebk.)
Subjects: LCSH: Toothpaste--Juvenile literature. | Oral hygiene products industry--Juvenile literature.
Classification: LCC TP955 .B47 2017 (print) | LCC TP955 (ebook) | DDC 668.1--dc23
LC record available at http://lccn.loc.gov/2016005666

Printed in the United States of America in Brainerd, Minnesota
1 2 3 4 5 6 7 8 9 0 20 19 18 17 16

072016
210716

Project Coordinator: John Willis   Art Director: Terry Paulhus

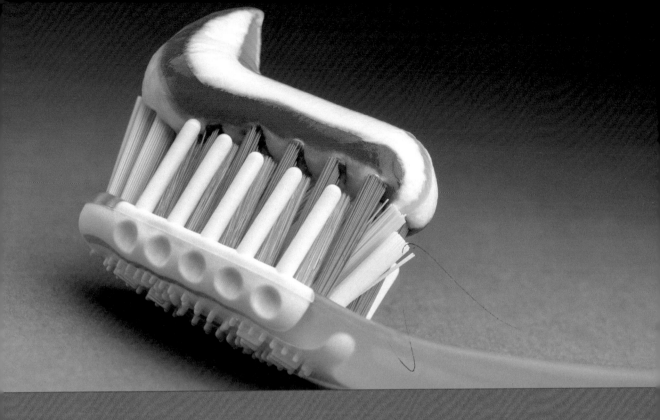

Contents

A Tooth Scrubber

Did you know that your teeth are cleaned with rocks? That may sound strange, but it is true. Some of these tiny rocks are called **abrasives**. These pieces of rock are much smaller than grains of sand. They are part of what makes toothpaste such a great tooth scrubber. Abrasives scratch and grind at the surface of something. They remove tiny pieces of food stuck in your teeth. They also take away **plaque** on the surface of teeth. Toothpaste has many other **ingredients**, too. Lots of these are made from minerals that come from rocks. Some ingredients make your teeth whiter. Some keep your breath smelling fresh. Together, they keep your teeth healthy and clean.

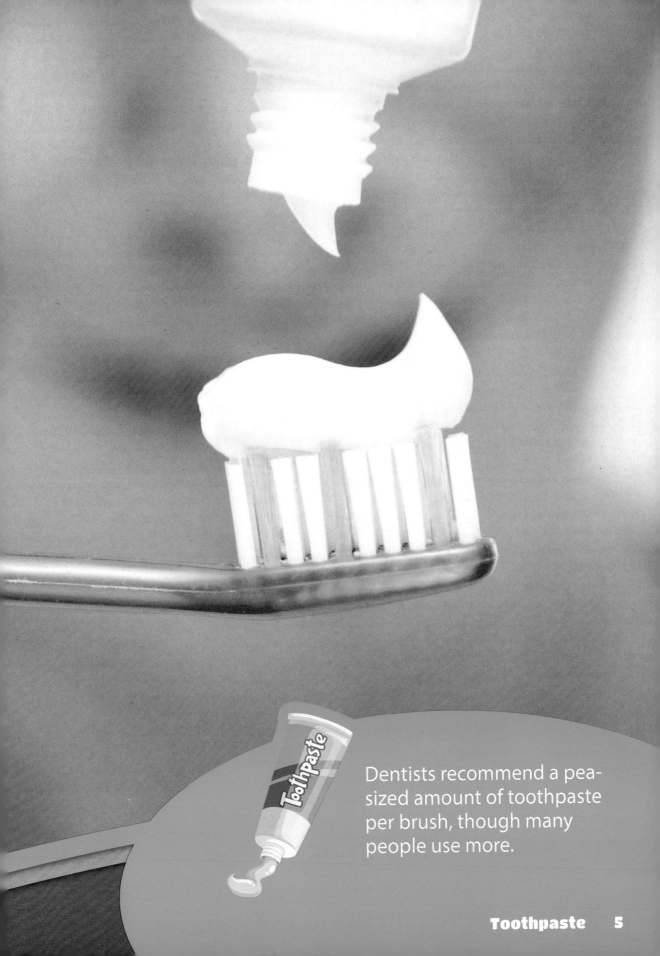

Dentists recommend a pea-sized amount of toothpaste per brush, though many people use more.

The four main ingredients of toothpaste are water, abrasives, fluoride, and detergents.

Have you thought about how toothpaste is made? First, the toothpaste factory buys **chemicals** used in the toothpaste. These chemicals are made in labs at chemical companies. Then, they are shipped to toothpaste factories in large bags or containers.

Now it is time to make the toothpaste. There are many steps. The first step starts with the toothpaste recipe. Every toothpaste company has its own special recipe. However, some things are common in all brands of toothpaste.

The Toothpaste Recipe

Abrasives are the power scrubbers in toothpaste. Binders are also needed. They make toothpaste smooth and thick. Binders keep the ingredients mixed together in a paste. That is important because it helps toothpaste stay on your toothbrush.

Sudsers are foaming bubbles. They help get rid of food pieces. Toothpaste needs a **humectant**. It keeps water in the toothpaste. The toothpaste stays moist, so it feels good in your mouth.

Sudsers help keep toothpaste from dribbling out of a person's mouth and down the chin.

Toothpaste needs to taste good so you will keep using it. Flavor oils add the fresh taste people like. The oils also help keep your breath smelling good. Some toothpaste companies use natural flavor oils. These oils are made from herbs such as peppermint.

Most large toothpaste companies use chemicals to make the oil. All flavor oils have both taste and smell. Fluoride is added to make your teeth strong. Whiteners are added to make your teeth look whiter. Whiteners work by getting rid of stains on tooth **enamel**.

A common abrasive is **chalk**. Chalk is a type of rock.

There are many different flavors of toothpaste, but the most popular is mint.

A Toothpaste Factory

The different ingredients are weighed and tested for quality. It is important that each ingredient is just right. First, water is mixed with the humectant in a large container called a mixing vat. The water and humectant then goes through pipes to another part of the factory. That part of the factory is called the make area. That is where the rest of the ingredients are added.

The ingredients are mixed together in a large vat. This vat is like a very large pot. Its lid has mixing blades. Some vats hold enough toothpaste to make 10,000 tubes.

Bigger vats hold enough toothpaste to make 30,000 tubes.

Workers add abrasives to the mix. If the abrasive is chalk, it goes into a giant sifter. This sifts out the big pieces, so only tiny pieces go into the toothpaste. Then, workers add sudsers and flavor oils to the mix. Some popular flavors are peppermint and cinnamon.

Most toothpaste has fluoride, which is added next. If the toothpaste is going to be a whitening type, then a whitener is also used. **Preservatives** are added so the toothpaste can stay on a store's shelf for a long time. Sweeteners are added to make the toothpaste taste good.

Finally, the ingredients are heated together inside the vat. The mixing blades move through the mixture. The toothpaste becomes smooth and shiny.

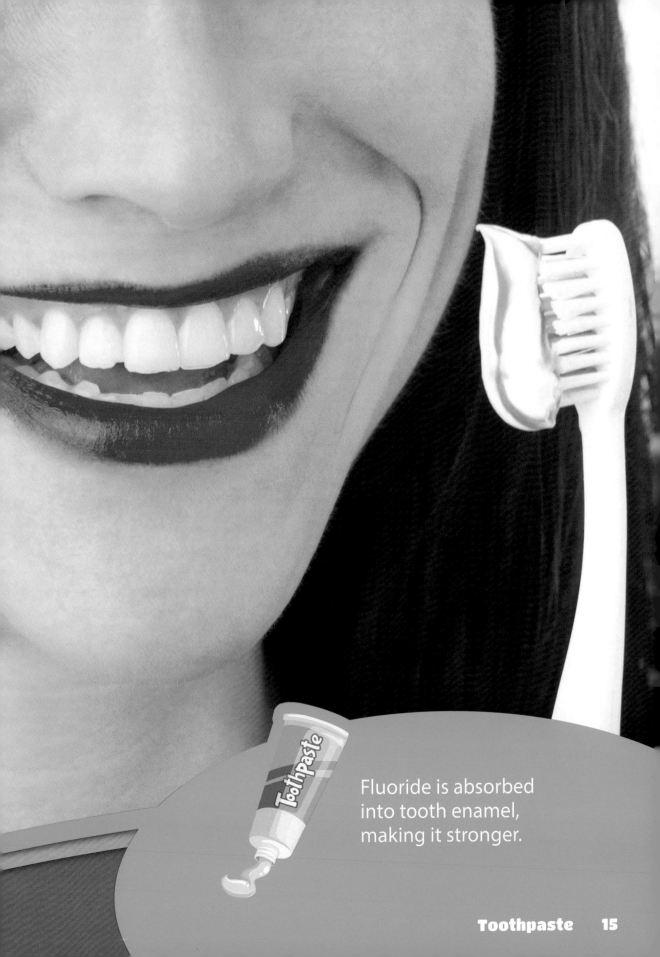

Fluoride is absorbed into tooth enamel, making it stronger.

Cleaning the toothpaste off
the blades is like cleaning
frosting off a really big mixer.

Cooling the Toothpaste

After the toothpaste has been mixed and heated, it has to be cooled. The toothpaste now looks like gooey dough. Workers raise the lid of the vat and scrape and clean the large mixing blades. None of the toothpaste is wasted. Next, workers test small samples of the toothpaste batch. The testers make sure each batch tastes good and is smooth. A machine also tests the toothpaste to make sure it has the right amount of water. A worker throws away batches that do not pass the tests.

A machine blows air into the tubes to remove dust before the toothpaste is added.

Filling the Tubes

Good batches of toothpaste can move on in the factory. The batches go through hoses to filling machines. These machines fill the toothpaste tubes.

First, workers put toothpaste tubes on a **conveyor belt**. The caps are already on, but the bottom is open. The tubes go to the filling machine with the cap side down. A machine holds the tube in place. Then, a filling machine squirts just enough toothpaste into each tube.

Many people like toothpaste with stripes. If the toothpaste is white, only one hose fills the toothpaste tubes. To make striped toothpaste, food coloring is added to white toothpaste. Then, a separate hose is used for each color. The hoses squirt their colors into a toothpaste tube at the same time. The stripes go from the cap to the end of the tube. Each time you brush, you will have striped toothpaste.

The tubes continue on the conveyor belt to the sealing machine. This machine pulls the ends of the tubes together. It folds them over and seals them. Finally, the tubes are stamped with the date the toothpaste **expires**. Toothpaste can go bad after a certain time. It will not clean your teeth as well as it should.

Striped toothpaste was invented in 1955.

Next, a machine paints the outside of the tube. It also adds labels to the tubes. A label tells important information about the toothpaste. The label includes the name of the toothpaste and the name of the company that made it. It also shows information about what the toothpaste was made to do. Some toothpaste is made to whiten teeth. Some helps stop **cavities** from forming. Many kinds of toothpaste do many jobs at the same time.

The machine that labels toothpaste tubes is very fast. It can label **150 tubes** or more every minute.

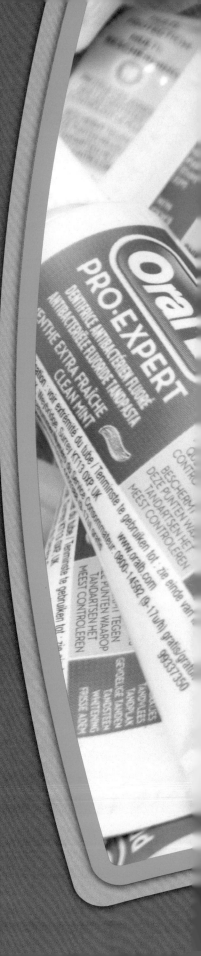

Toothpaste makers are required to put safety information on the outside of the tube.

Inspectors make sure the right number of tubes go into packing boxes.

Tested and Boxed

Next, the conveyor belt takes the tubes to an inspector. This worker looks at each tube and pulls out any that are not perfect. Sometimes the label may not have gone on the right way, or the tube may have a hole in it. A machine weighs the tubes. The weight shows if the right amount of toothpaste is inside.

Tubes that are not perfect are not thrown away. Many times they are sold to companies that sell seconds. Seconds are items that have something wrong with them. The box might not be perfect or the color may be wrong. People who buy seconds pay much less for the items.

In stores, toothpaste is often sold in individual boxes.

The tubes that pass inspection are boxed. Some companies do this packing by hand. Others do it with machines. The boxes are weighed to make sure each box has the right number of tubes in it. Then, the boxes are sealed and stored in the factory's warehouse. The toothpaste is now ready to be shipped to the store.

Onto Your Brush

Toothpaste ships by trucks to neighborhood stores. The new toothpaste tubes might go to a grocery store, a drug store, or a department store. Toothpaste can even be sold at gas stations.

You have lots of choices when you shop for toothpaste. What yummy flavor do you want? Do you want stripes? What do you want your toothpaste to do? Do you want your teeth whiter? Do you want them stronger? Pick a toothpaste you like. Remember to brush your teeth every day. You will have a mouthful of happy, healthy teeth.

People should brush their teeth twice a day.

Quiz

Match the steps with the pictures.

A. Ingredients mixed.

B. Batch is cooled

C. Tubes filled

D. Inspector checks tubes

E. Ship to store

F. Onto your brush

Answers
1.B 2.C 3.A 4.F 5.E 6.D

Key Words

abrasives: materials that are rough and can be used to grind something else

cavities: holes in teeth that can be prevented by using toothpaste

chemicals: substances made using chemistry

conveyor belt: a moving belt that takes materials from one place to another in a factory

enamel: the hard, white surface of teeth

expires: when something reaches the end of the time it can be used

humectant: a material that keeps moisture in something

ingredients: things that are added to a mixture, like items in a recipe list

plaque: a film of bacteria, food, and saliva that is found on the surface of a tooth and can hurt teeth

preservatives: chemicals added to foods and drinks to keep them from spoiling

Index

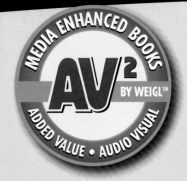

Log on to www.av2books.com

AV² by Weigl brings you media enhanced books that support active learning. Go to www.av2books.com, and enter the special code found on page 2 of this book. You will gain access to enriched and enhanced content that supplements and complements this book. Content includes video, audio, weblinks, quizzes, a slide show, and activities.

AV² Online Navigation

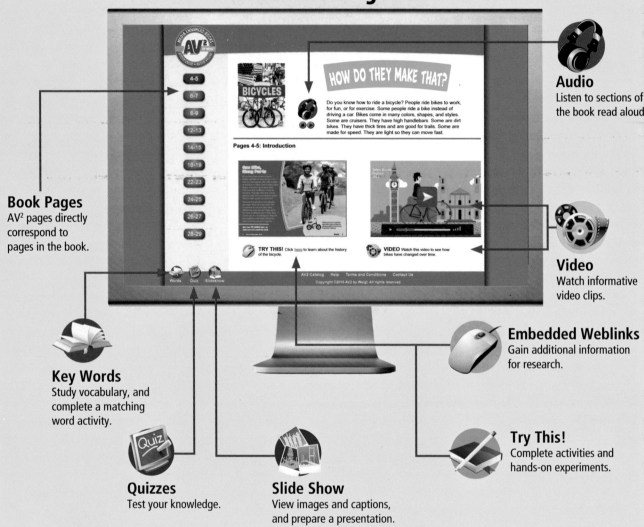

Book Pages
AV² pages directly correspond to pages in the book.

Audio
Listen to sections of the book read aloud

Video
Watch informative video clips.

Embedded Weblinks
Gain additional information for research.

Key Words
Study vocabulary, and complete a matching word activity.

Try This!
Complete activities and hands-on experiments.

Quizzes
Test your knowledge.

Slide Show
View images and captions, and prepare a presentation.

AV² was built to bridge the gap between print and digital. We encourage you to tell us what you like and what you want to see in the future.

Sign up to be an AV² Ambassador at www.av2books.com/ambassador.